Cute and Cuddly: Baby Animals

BABY KOALAS

By Katie Kawa

Gareth Stevens
Publishing

Please visit our website, www.garethstevens.com. For a free color catalog of all our high-quality books, call toll free 1-800-542-2595 or fax 1-877-542-2596.

Library of Congress Cataloging-in-Publication Data

Kawa, Katie.
Baby koalas / Katie Kawa.
    p. cm. — (Cute and cuddly: baby animals)
ISBN 978-1-4339-5528-0 (pbk.)
ISBN 978-1-4339-5529-7 (6-pack)
ISBN 978-1-4339-5526-6 (library binding)
1. Koala—Infancy—Juvenile literature. I. Title.
QL737.M384K39 2011
599.2'5139—dc22

                                    2010050028

First Edition

Published in 2012 by
Gareth Stevens Publishing
111 East 14th Street, Suite 349
New York, NY 10003

Copyright © 2012 Gareth Stevens Publishing

Editor: Katie Kawa
Designer: Andrea Davison-Bartolotta

Photo credits: Cover, pp. 11, 15 iStockphoto.com; pp. 1, 5 Ian Waldie/Getty Images; p. 7 Delia Anthony/ Getty Images; pp. 9, 24 (pouch) James Hager/Getty Images; pp. 13, 17, 19, 23, 24 (fur) Shutterstock.com; p. 21 David McNew/Getty Images.

Printed in the United States of America

CPSIA compliance information: Batch #CR213110GS: For further information contact Gareth Stevens, New York, New York at 1-800-542-2595.

Contents

Babies and Mothers 4

Life in Trees 14

Eating and Sleeping 18

Words to Know 24

Index. 24

A baby koala is called a joey.

A baby koala is the size of a jelly bean. It cannot see or hear.

A baby koala lives in its mother's pouch. It stays there for six months.

Then, a baby koala rides on its mother's back.

Koalas have gray fur.
Their ears are big
and fuzzy.

Baby koalas live in trees.

Baby koalas have strong hands and feet. These help them climb.

A baby koala has a big nose. This helps it smell food.

Baby koalas eat leaves.

Baby koalas sleep all day.

Words to Know

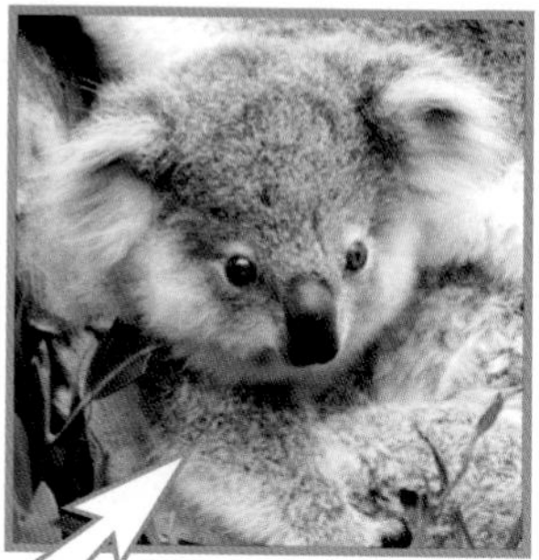

fur

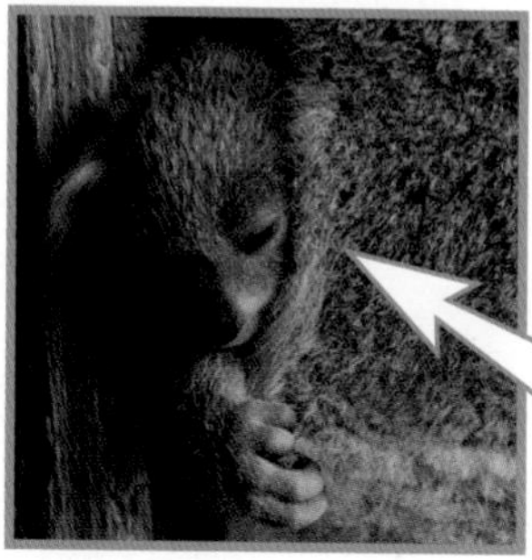

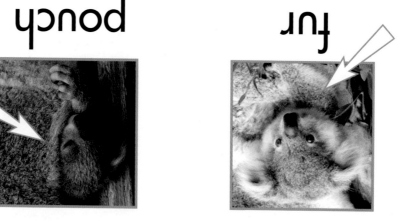

pouch

Index

fur 12
joey 4
pouch 8
trees 14

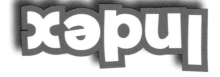